ANGEL GUIDANCE

FOR

AWAKENING

SPIRITUAL GIFTS

Uncover your natural ability

Angel Guidance For Awakening Spiritual Gifts

Uncover your natural ability

Z.Z. Rae

Other Books by Z.Z. Rae

Your Voice Your Choice: *The Value of Every Woman*

Ties of the Heart: How to recover from Divorce and Breakups *(A 12 step-by-step healing process)*

I Want to be a Unicorn *(Why Unicorns are Real and You can be One*

Angel Guidance Series

Angel Guidance for Wealth *(Abundant living for everyone)*

Angel Guidance for *Dreams (Your dreams explained by the angels)*

Angel Guidance for Inner Healing *(Heal your heart, soul, and mind with the angels)*

Angel Guidance for Creativity *(Unlock your gift)*

Angel Guidance for Peace *(Allow life's burdens to fade)*

Angel Guidance for Joy *(Raise your vibrations)*

Angel Guidance for Energy Healing *(Aligning your beliefs with your desires)*

Angel Guidance for Awakening Spiritual Gifts *(Uncover your natural ability)*

Spiritual Tools

How to Work with Archangels: *(Guidance from archangels for abundance, healing, spiritual wisdom, and more.)*

Books by Natasha House

Grace Alive Series

Christian Romance

Grace Alive

Grace Unbroken

Rebirth of the Prophesy Series

Sci-fi Romance

Fatal Alien Affection (FREE)

Fatal Alien Attraction (was Citizen)

The Jade Series

Epic Fantasy

The Vullens' Curse

The Deities' Touch

The Vision Stone

Super Hero Princess Series

Middle grade/Young Adult

Zara (was Superhero Princess and the Curse of the Rainbow Fairy)

Non-Fiction

How to KEEP Writing Your Book

Illustrated Sermons for Youth or Adults

Grace Speaks

For my beautiful Grandma Joyce Spohn

Chapter 1: Breathe

Angel Makaia

Start off by taking a nice, big, deep breath. Hold it in for five seconds, and then release it slowly. Do it again. Connect with your breath, and allow it to travel from the top of your head all the way down. Feel the breath going through your entire body and softening you on the inside. Release all the striving and fear about not understanding your spiritual gifting and awakening. Let yourself just be in this moment, right here, right now. That's good. Take another one now. Allow the breath to travel to a place inside of you which feels deeply afraid that you don't have what it takes to be 'special' or to hold a gift inside of you.

Allow that breath to travel to that place of fear, and allow it to draw it to the surface of your heart, and out into your exhale. Once you've done this, keep breathing, until you feel the fear has released. The fear of failure is buried inside almost every single human heart. The fear withholds your true self from really taking form in this world. You can become afraid that others are better, or that you aren't where you should be with your spiritual awakening. You may feel, as you look back, that you were slow, or that you wished you would have learned a bit faster. Release all of those things you hold inside of you. Breathe. Breathe it out.

Close your eyes for a moment, and picture a moth. I know that doesn't sound very pleasant, but I want you to see yourself as this moth. Floating around, not exactly sure what it is doing. In your mind's eye, see this moth transform into a beautiful creature. Spread those wings wider, and see color dancing on the surface of them. Look out over the world, and see yourself with the capacity to *fly*. Now, look at that beautiful creature you are becoming and laugh. Laugh in the beauty of who your true nature is right now. Don't see yourself as a dull moth, but rather see yourself as this transforming beautiful thing which is flying high.

This is step one to awakening. Awaken the fear. Let it come up. Release the fear. How do you truly understand yourself unless you face that fear? How can you truly wake up without knowing your deepest fears and desires that are always under the surface of your soul? Just allow it to be. Allow the fear to come, and then you can identify its source, and get to the bottom of things inside of you. That is the first key to awakening. Acknowledging what is and discovering what will be.

Prayer

Father,

Thank you for waking me up to my true self. Help me to see my true nature is beautiful. I allow the fear to come, so that I can release it, and truly know who I am. Amen.

Chapter 2: Body

Angel Monafia

This is one of my favorite subjects to help aid with. In order to truly awaken from your sense of slumber, you must become aware of your body sensations. Many of you stuff down the feelings your body is trying to tell you, and as a result, it resists you. For example, if you are facing an ache in your body, and you don't know how to restore it back to health, you must first accept that the pain is there. Acknowledge that you realize it is trying to speak to you, and then discover the underlining issue that your body is trying to express.

The body does not do things to hurt you. It is simply trying to speak a big, loud message that something you're doing is bringing it discomfort. So, if you are working too hard or becoming far too negative for its liking, it responds with *pain*. Think of it much like a little baby. All that baby knows to tell you what it needs is to *cry*. Of course, crying isn't very comfortable for you or that baby, but that is the only thing it knows to do to tell you what it needs.

So is the body. You can get to a place, just as a little baby, where facial expressions, sounds, or even a feeling can communicate far easier. The body doesn't always have to simply give you pain to talk to you. You will notice different things over time, and when you are heeding your body's messages, you'll start to notice more and more about other things in your life. You start to get into a place of awareness. Do not treat your body like it is something to be abhorred or annoyed at. Simply tell your body, "I hear you. What are you trying to tell me?"

Be sensitive to the needs of your body—just as you would a small child. Allow it to talk to you, and then understand there are things it needs in order to feel safe, secure, happy, and loved. Your body is the second step to overcome your fears, worries, and stresses about not understanding your gift. When you can tune into your body, pretty soon you can tune into others' needs as well. This will help you have deep compassion, empathy, as well as insight into circumstances, that you would not have otherwise had.

Sensitivity to one's own body is important to overcoming obstacles in one's life. If you can master yourself first, then you will truly be open and aware of way more. Here is a little thing I want you to do. Lie flat. Or if you are more comfortable sitting, do so. Now, just feel. Feel where discomfort is in your body. Settle your awareness on that area, and I want you to acknowledge it to yourself. Tell your body, "I hear you." Now that you have become aware of that area of need, simply ask your body why it is in a place of discomfort.

You may get several kinds of feelings or senses. This takes practice. Don't be mad at yourself for not knowing what's wrong. Just accept that you don't know, and allow the feeling to be. Love the feeling, and then accept yourself for all of the pains and feelings. This will open up your senses, and your body will know *I'm safe*. When you refuse to acknowledge the body's messages, it soon becomes much like a child. It will throw a bigger, much harsher tantrum. All of that could have been avoided if you'd heeded your body at the start of what it was trying to tell you.

Don't fret about this. Just tell yourself you hear, see, and feel what it wants. You may not know all of the answers yet, but you can still at least accept the feeling as it is. There is freedom in doing that right now. Once you can be aware of your body, you'll know how to start working on your energy and emotions to bring enlightenment to yourself. First, acknowledge your own self before trying to enlighten others.

Prayer

Father,

Thank you for helping me understand my own body. I know you'll help me heal and acknowledge my own self. Amen.

Chapter 3: Inward Journey

Angel Gabriel

Beginning the journey inside of yourself can be quite a terrifying experience. The next step to awakening is to face your biggest obstacles and to overcome them. Recognizing the struggle, you may face within yourself, can be a challenge. Many times, people deny what is right in front of them, and turn away from it. It is time to face it. Head on. This is how you will engage with your spiritual senses in full force. You mustn't run away from them. You mustn't hide from your senses. You have to be able to fully use these in order to operate on a much higher frequency level.

Before you can tap into the newness of who you truly are on the inside, you'll need to clear away a lot of the old energy. Face your demons, so to speak, and you'll be able to help others face theirs as well. Don't be afraid to speak your mind. Don't be afraid to show the truth. Don't be afraid to be yourself in front of others. When you hide away, hide away, hide away, you'll never understand the true expression of who you are.

Who is to say you are in the wrong and the other is in the right? Or who is to say you are in the right and they are in the wrong? When you flat out label things such as that, then you're absolutely missing the whole point of life. You are not living. You are being in a state of right and wrong, and you are judging that which is not your right to judge. You are not created to be judge and jury over yourself or others. When you step into the place of judgement like that, you dampen your true nature. You actually turn off everything inside of you and become something you're not—judgement. If the maker of the entire universe doesn't judge, why does a simple human form think they have the right to judge as well?

The spirits all continue to get agitated at times over the human ego—the condition greatly abhors them, but we remind them that the human ego is a learning system for all. We long to pull the human condition into a higher state of consciousness. We long for them to become aware of their condition, so they face it, instead of running and hiding, running and hiding. The spirits are aware of this running and hiding, and it puzzles them, because they don't understand why anyone would hide from their very self! They find it quite strange how humans are in that state every day.

I suppose it is like contracting a virus. They don't even realize that the actual virus is not who they are, but it is something which has attacked them. If the human condition can understand that the egocentric self is simply something to release and not hang onto, they'd be much more aware and joyful in their daily lives.

It is simply about trust—awareness—and love. Love is the foundation to the universe, and it will always be. There is nothing contradicting love in our eyes. There is no greater power in the vastness of time, space, and existence than the power of love. Nothing can come against it and win. Love is powerful. The powerlessness of life only stems from the lack of love in some area. If you are struggling in any area, you must ask yourself, "Where is my love for this? Am I in a state of love here?" If your answer is simply, "No." Then that is the reason for the suffering. The state of love is your natural state. That is why you suffer. Because love has run away, or in your eyes it has. Because, simply enough, you are running away from yourself, because you are love too.

The universe was based on one principle—love. So, if you are coming up against love, and not allowing love, or fearing love, then you are not in the state of allowing the system in the universe to work in its proper form. You are resisting love; resisting existence in itself. By going against love, you are pushing up against a wall, which cannot be moved. You cannot break love. You cannot move it. It will stay and always remain. Ask a mother of a child. Ask her if the love she has ever leaves or breaks away. Ask her if she would still die for her child, even if that child is a full-grown woman. You will see the ultimate power of love.

Prayer

Father,

Thank you for showing me the power of love. Your love is so deep for me. You based your entire universe on love, and I choose to stay in love in my life. Amen.

Chapter 4: Existence

I'd like to take a moment to speak about existence. Existence must be allowed in order to awaken to your true self. If you are not allowing true existence, in yourself, you will have a hell of a time. Excuse my verbiage, but you will. If you are constantly battling the state of *being,* within your own sense of awareness, you will not be able to open up to the true nature of who you are.

You are fighting that which is supposed to be embraced. It is not your job to stand up for yourself, fight the power, and constantly wrestle against everyone and everything. That is plain out exhausting. Don't look at me funny when I say not to stand up for yourself. It is not that you allow others to walk over you. It is simply to get into a state of just being YOU. When you are in a state of you—you do not need to 'stand up for yourself', because you are already being yourself. At that point, there is nothing to stand up for. You are simply allowing yourself room to be.

You don't need to fight against another's opinion of you, because you'll recognize that you are already in a state of allowing, and you don't need them to show you how to 'be' or who to 'be'. You have already discovered the being without them. This is another key to be awakened unto yourself. You don't look outside of yourself for the answer to all life's little crazy questions. You simply *be,* and the answer arrives in your heart. It knows.

Now you're looking at me even more funny, because you wonder how to just be in that state of allowing. It's simply allowing yourself to connect to that state of oneness or *being.* Ah, now we're going to hard ball with this subject. You are a form—or some would even say a formula of existence. The fact that you exist here and now is your choice. You came here to exist, and you must *allow* that existence to happen. You must say to yourself, "I am here to exist, and it is good." When you get into the allowing of existing, nothing else will matter so much as simply being *alive* in this time and season. You don't need to excuse yourself for being or existing. It is your RIGHT to exist here. It is your call to exist here in the now moment.

Don't be afraid of that existence either. For in that existing, is where you'll find your true sense of self or nature. It's in this moment. You don't have to wrestle with others to exist. You have all the power to exist, and they must leave it at that. You have your own choices in this existence too. They cannot control that. You do. If it seems your existence is very difficult, or trying at all times, that is because your state of being is creating that very taxing state.

No one creates that for you. You do. Because you are a being that exists, and in that existence, it is creating what it wants to do. So, if you allow others to boss you around in that existence, that is also your choice to exist that way. Is this making some sense?

Allow yourself to exist. Be. Stop trying so hard to do something you're not. Your gifts are there; stop trying to absorb someone else's gifts. That's not the thing which will make you happy inside. Just being will. Just being you. Exist!

Prayer

Father,

You have created me to exist, and I choose to be happy in that. I choose to follow my heart, and allow myself to express freely. Amen.

Chapter 5: Kindness

Angel Jamel

Kindness. We want to touch on kindness. Mostly with yourself. You are pressuring yourself so much to uncover your gift, that it is putting strain on you. Strain can cause more pain, and the pain can dampen what we want to awaken. Once you are fully in tune with yourself, you awaken to your full capacity. How do you awaken to your true self? One step at a time, and each of those steps is filled with treating yourself with love and kindness. Don't look at yourself and think, "Why isn't it happening? What am I doing wrong?" You are doing nothing wrong. Your gift is already there, you just have to be patient and kind to yourself to fully understand it's workings.

Treat yourself as you deserve to be treated. With love, patience, kindness, and understanding. Look at yourself with compassion each day. When you wake up, smile, and give yourself a genuine hug. It does something to you deep inside. Each time you recognize who you truly are, not just what you think you are, or what people have spoken over you, you'll bring your true essence into existence. Your gift won't be difficult to activate, because you'll understand yourself in a greater degree. In order to truly walk it out, you must first walk it out with connection, love, compassion, and kindness toward yourself. Everyone falls short; everyone does something they later regret, but it's all in how you view yourself afterward that has a lasting impact. Keep looking at yourself with a compassionate view—a kind view. Look at yourself as you would a child you adore. That child is bound to make mistakes and hurt you at times, but deep inside, you know they love you, and you love them back as well.

Treat yourself with kindness today.

Prayer

Father,

Thank you for showing me how to treat myself with love, compassion, and kindness. You always look at me with love, and I choose to look at myself that way too. Amen.

Chapter 6: Tune In

Angel Mallory

Often times people look at themselves with a hyper-critical eye. Do you see every flaw, fault, mishap, and burp you make? A critical eye toward yourself will always lead to disconnection. When you criticize anyone, it leads to a gap between the two of you—whether you do it mentally or spoken. Think of it this way. If you had a best friend, who you suddenly found out was critical of you, or a person you knew was constantly putting you down, wouldn't you have a disconnection with that person? You may even feel deep sadness, because you love them—such as a parent. But, because of their criticism toward you, you cannot feel connected to them in a safe way. This is also the case within yourself. If you don't feel safe opening up to yourself, you will never fully experience the gift of who you are. Your inner self will never express, because it feels judged, cut down, and sad. You must first deeply love, accept, and appreciate every part of yourself. This causes openness and connection in multiple ways.

Taking the time to listen to yourself is key to opening up yourself more to your spiritual gifting. If you are constantly shutting down your own voice because you feel lack or feelings of disapproval over yourself, you'll have a much more challenging time truly operating in your spiritual gift. There is a bridge from your true self to the natural world. If you can learn to cross it, in a healthy manner, you'll feel, see, and experience the spiritual gift you have always had. Every human, on this planet, has a deep gift within. Most of these gifts are to bring love, life, and joy to each other, and some are to aid deeper issues in the earth—such as the actual nature surrounding everyone.

Do not discredit your own ability. This also leads to disconnection between your inner being and outer world.

Think of it this way. Whenever you have a disapproving thought about yourself, you are putting up a stone wall with your true self and manifestation. When you feel *bad* it's usually because you are at discord with your true self. When you can release the negative things about yourself, or your lack of self, then you can truly open up to a spiritual gift inside of you. Some of you have more than one, and we want to also express that sometimes the variety of gifts you carry can seem a bit overwhelming. Focus in on the one that is currently drawing you, and the other ones will fall into place as you go. It doesn't have to be a struggle to operate in your gift with others. If you feel as if you have always struggled and struggled, and have often times thought, *I don't think I'm special or gifted,* then we want to say to you that this is your problem. Your struggle. Your unwanted emotions and thoughts. These have created the wall between your true self and manifestation.

We know it is hard to let go of past experiences many times, but in order to activate the things needed in your life, you must stop giving attention to those past experiences. What do I mean by that? It simply means, the more thought, expression, and energy you give to the disappointments, the more the disappointments will come and manifest once again. Once you give attention to the positives in your life, the more the positives will start to develop. So, we want to give you the steps such as in A...B...C..., but we are showing you the steps if you listen intently to our words.

Regrets are slowing you down. Fear is slowing you down. Old past experiences are slowing you down. Once you stop looking at those so much, you'll start to see the truth of who you are. You are a being of light. A being of joy. A pure essence of love to this earth. That is your true nature, and the more you can become in-tuned with that side of you, the better. Blessings on all of you!

Prayer

Father,

Thank you for showing me how to tune into the true me. Help me not criticize myself any longer. I am beautifully and wonderfully made. You created me that way. Amen.

Chapter 7: Matters of the Heart

Angel Jamel

Healing begins in the heart. The heart can be one of the scariest things for most to really truly look at. Many people hide from their own heart, because it's far too painful to look at their heart's damage. The experiences in the heart is what turns your life one way or another. Many people will say the mind is the strongest of all functions, but if the heart is pulling against the mind, the heart will win out in the end. That is why people will say, "This relationship is what I want, but I can't seem to put my heart into it." Or they will say, "I like this, but I don't have the heart to do it." Many people say these types of phrases, and it just seems to be a phrase to them. What they don't realize is that the heart is dictating their actions many times.

The heart has many places stored inside. In those storage areas are what we'd call *life experiences*, and in those experiences, many find either love or feelings of mistrust. The more life experiences they gain with mistrust, the harder it is for them to open those specific doors in their life.

For example: if there are many heart experiences with the area of relationships, so that they are closed to new ones, or they simply keep reopening the same door and reliving the same heart condition, then nothing changes. Once they revisit those doors, deal with the pain of that experience, and realize that they are no longer living in that specific experience, then things start to look differently. The heart must be in union with you when it comes to your spiritual awakening. If you have had many doors of disappointment concerning your gifting, you will find the heart does not want to work with you. If you can look at those experiences as lessons and learn from them, then you can open new doors for your awakening.

You must work with the heart not against it. It will always win out in the end.

Prayer

Father,

Thank you for showing me how to work with my own heart and let go of the past experiences. I choose to open my heart back up again. Amen.

Chapter 8: Steps

Angel Dedication

We know this name seems very odd to you, so we want to explain why we chose the name dedication. You're trying to pull on things which appear as if they are 'hard, difficult, or impossible' for your living experience. We want to show you that there is a deep need inside all of you to dedicate yourself to this task. The problem is the more you strive to be awakened, the more you seem to be further from the mark! Why does that seem to be so? We wish to explain a few principles of what we know to do.

Dedication to your own self is very vital, though we know you wish to help aid others in your spiritual journey. Of course, you will be a light and healing principle to others, but first you must say to yourself, "I am dedicated to my own passion." You must first choose to be free from thinking or obligation of what others are expecting of you to do. You are often times fighting your own power. You are fighting against yourself at such an extreme rate, that we are trying to get you to see what you are doing. Many of you were raised in a way that your parents or family members were always right. You couldn't seem to understand why you wanted to go one way, when they desired you to go an extreme opposite. This is because you have a different soul purpose than the souls around you.

It can be a bigger challenge for those who are striving against people who they care about. Their soul is trying to speak to them their life's purpose, but their conscious mind or the way they were conditioned is speaking another way. That can lead to their soul in turmoil. If you feel weird, different, or strive with those around you, understand that your deeper purpose is trying to fight its way to the surface of your consciousness.

If it seems you are drawn to abnormal paths, or teachings that isn't what you were raised with, then understand it is for a purpose and time. Do not worry so much about what others' will think of you. If they are supposed to be a part of your soul's purpose, they will be. If not, they won't. It is as simple as that. Some are for a time and a reason, and others are for a season. Do not beat yourself up over it.

Prayer

Father,

Thank you for leading me, and helping me along my life's journey. I trust that you will show me the steps to take in order to get to where I need to go in life. Amen.

Chapter 9: Trust

Angel Kale

The trust cycle is easily broken. You build trust and then it becomes shattered by someone you hold close to you. When you are awakening to yourself, you must restore trust within yourself. If you are questioning your own choices, views, and beliefs about yourself, you will have a harder time seeing yourself for who you are.

As life moves forward, you may see yourself as one who makes dumb mistakes, or you may feel as if you don't do anything that is pleasing. This is where you must look beyond the so called mistakes and learn from what you have gone through. Once you do this, you must allow yourself to restore trust within yourself. If you are consciously always trusting others to run your life, you will have a life of frustration and ignorance. While others can give you tips and advice, and often times wisdom to aid you, you must search for the deeper source within you and begin to learn and grow from that source. Father created you with an essence to love who you are and those around you. If you learn from that essence, you will see how loved you truly are.

Don't fear the mistakes you have so called made in your life. If it brought you to where you need to go, then you were in the right place at the right time. Even if this so called experience felt very bad to you. When you walk away from it, you can now look and see that you want to choose a better physical experience for your life. So was the bad so bad? If it led you to the good? Would you have gotten there without the so called bad experience?

This is what you must look at. Learning to trust yourself is vital to awakening yourself. If you are not trusting the little signs and senses you are getting, you will not understand how to fully open up to those signs and senses. If you find yourself dismissing things in a manner such as, "That's nothing. I don't think that was a big deal." The signs won't help you learn to open up further and further to more spiritual things.

Perhaps you feel very distracted by life—there is always a crisis or a fire to put out at every corner. Are you simply distracting yourself from your true purpose? Are you trying to excuse working on the trust that you so desire within yourself? If you often think, "But, I have been wrong so many times." You must understand that the wrongness of the situation led you to the rightness of a new one, so was it indeed wrong or right?

We know this is very boggling to your mind sometimes. This is how we want to help you understand not to avoid yourself. Do not avoid trusting yourself with life. Because, even the so called "wrong" led you to the so called "right." And that is what we want you to look at in a healthy way. Even if the experience you have now doesn't feel pleasing to you, you'll need to look beyond that. Let it ride you to the experience you so desire.

We will give you an example again. Say you have dated what you'd call *bad guys,* and over time you finally said within yourself, "I am done with this." So, you began to work on your inner being, beliefs, and started to let go of the baggage of the bad guys. Are these bad guys so bad now? They led you to the belief within yourself that you needed to work out the baggage and the pain from the experiences of the past. Are these experiences now deemed bad or good? Ha, now we know you are thinking. There isn't one experience in your existence that doesn't lead you to a new one. If you are looping the same bad-feeling experience, that is why we want to help you get out of that bad-feeling, and into a new one soon. For, the more you give attention to that bad-feeling experience, it seems to keep happening in your life.

Learn from it and grow.

Prayer

Father,

Thank you for turning my bad feeling experiences into good. You work all things together for my good. Thank you for showing me lessons from the experiences I've faced. Amen.

Chapter 10: Desires

Angel Malachi

There are many desires stirring inside of you, and I wish to discuss this with you. Many times, you do what we call 'bounce therapy'. We call it therapy, because you exercise different aspects of yourself. You find things you exercise a bit here and a bit there, but often times you say to us, "Why am I not growing any further ahead? Why do I feel I keep going in the same places, and not advancing any steps?" This is because your bouncing therapy is in a circle, and you are not choosing an avenue in which to ride forward or move! We see you bounce, bounce, bounce, between the same things, because you aren't desiring something in yourself strong enough to take the steps out into the world.

This bouncing can be a period of waiting or correlating what you truly want to do. This isn't a negative thing to do in oneself. The bouncing can help uncover or discover what you desire, before you go in feet first. When you bounce first, before running out and achieving that which you desire, it can save much energy, time, and healing.

You ask us, "How do I know what my spiritual gift even is? I keep wondering and trying new things!" This is what we'd say to you, little ones. You are in a season of *bouncing,* and in that time, you must first ask yourself, "What feels best for my life?" Cause, sometimes others say, "This is what you are best at, and you should stick with it." Then we hear you say, "But, I don't know, because I like this too." That is because you are trying to get your feet wet in many things. In doing so, we are nodding our heads, because we see that your gifting has taken many formulas, and you are deciding which one you'd like to bring to yourself and others in this physical world.

You must ask yourself as you bounce, bounce, bounce, what you feel as you bounce. If you feel one bounce is very good, but you don't feel it 'sticks', then bounce again. If it feels even better, and it feels it 'sticks', explore that more. You will find attraction to certain avenues that will light you up, and others feel like a flicker or fizz. This isn't because it was wrong, bad, or not real, it just means that it was not what you need to attract inside at the moment. Gather and retrieve if you feel the need to do so. If you feel you aren't sure what will really make you fly, start with gathering that which makes you feel like flying. The more you feed the need to fly, the more you'll find yourself going toward the action and direction of flying. Does that make sense?

Gathering or as we say, bounce therapy, isn't good nor bad, it is a season of trying and finding. We see some give up after they've bounced around too long. That is because their energy, in their soul, needs to find a way to fly. If the bouncing happens too long and the soul feels ready to go in its direction, it will grow weary of the ground.

So, do not despise the bouncing! Bounce, bounce, bounce, but do go where you feel drawn or where it feels it 'sticks' inside.

Prayer

Father,

Thank you for helping me with the bouncing period going on in my life. I know you'll help me understand where I should go, and what feels right for my life. Amen.

Chapter 11: Distractions

Angel Mallory

Many things are swirling around you. Like tiny little lights that are flickering here and flickering there. At times, you are distracted by them, and you often wonder what they are for. You ask, "Why am I focused on this little thing here, instead of this bigger thing I really want over here?"

The little lights keep distracting you, and in a sense, calling to you to gather them. The little lights are a source of energy which is needed to be able to handle a more powerful light source that we want to hand to you. For if we launched you into the big sources, you'd find yourself wondering how to deal with it properly. You'd most likely doubt your capacity to handle that kind of power. This is the reason we show you the little flickering lights first. Understanding the little points of power is the first step. In doing so, we then see you are ready and able to handle even bigger points of power.

We know you are able to handle the bigger sources, but you don't always think you're able or ready, so you hesitate. We wish to help build the emotions inside of you to handle that which is flowing stronger. Many of you feel as if you are very *weak* in your abilities or gifts, but this is not the case. It is simply you are at a point where you think you're weaker, and so we give you the little lights, and not the bigger ones. We want to help you shuffle and handle those little points first before we draw you to the bigger ones. Make sense? Practice the little lights first. Are you understanding what I say by little lights? Ah, I will explain in a deeper realm. The little lights are *bursts* or energy that you can gather to you. These bursts will help you along your life's journey quite often.

If you were trying to handle the larger forms of energy, before you could handle it, you'd often feel very heavy, burdened, or unable to cope at times. Not that this energy feels bad, mind you, but your capacity to handle the stronger energy, to your physical form, would feel like that. If you feel as if sometimes your body is vibrating too fast—expressed in the form of anxiety at times—we will help you gather to yourself the smaller sources first. You can always say, "This is too much too fast." We will help you by sharing the load and gathering something at a much smaller scale. The more you feel you understand, the more powerful of a source will come to you. It isn't just an understanding, mind you, it is also an acceptance of yourself in a deeper way.

You are a powerful, light-filled being, that runs on pure energy. Even though you see yourself as in a physical bodily form, you also must understand that even that physical form is just millions of tiny points of energy all collected into one spot. This is how these tiny points of lights are all around you, and you can gather them. You can cause expansion within yourself by gathering the lights, and they will stick to your already high energy form.

You must also understand that we are never withholding a spiritual gift from you or teasing you with it. We know how you think and feel, and we understand if you are ready or not to handle more energy flow. If you have gathered much energy or these tiny points, we also know you must have an outflow, or it will be a lot for your physical form to handle. This is why we try to help you with the abilities as you feel you can handle them. This is a process for you, and you must know that as you grow to handle the bigger points of attraction of energy, you'll also be required to outsource more. Does that make sense? It's not about gathering bigger energy than your neighbor, but the more you gather, the more you'll feel a burden or a feeling to release it to the world to aid in healing others.

If you are a gatherer of these points of light, it is vital for your wellbeing to have an avenue of expression. Even though you may feel as if the things you gather are so very small, if you continue to gather them, you'll need a point of release. Don't feel as if what you are gathering is useless or pointless or feels too small. You will gather, and you will grow. As you grow, you'll feel attracted to a higher point of energy.

Prayer

Father,

Thank you for showing me the different points of energy I can gather to me. Thank you for helping me know that everything I do has its reward. I choose to grow and help myself and others. Amen.

Chapter 12: The Past

Angel Josheia

Mangled things can get in the way sometimes between gifts and you. What I am meaning by that is, there is sometimes old *wrecks* that are blocking your spiritual journey from happening to its fullest degree. There can be old energy forms that have gotten all gunked up, mangled, and blocked the way of your path. There are a few ways in which to let the gift flow in a stronger, more pure way. First of all, stop trying to go backward and fix that mangled gunk. That will not fix the flow at all. Instead, it will only add to the mangled gunk that's back there, because you'll be reattaching to it and flowing backward into that old energy. So, first off, stop looking at it. It's not going to change the fact that things got gunked up, mangled, and in the way of your path.

Once you stop looking backward, then we can work on the forward motion with you. Is this to say that we don't help clear the path from the past, no. We definitely help clear up the old mindsets, because if not, it'd be really hard to get you to see the clarity of the path before you. Giving constant focus to the 'been there done that' is not going to aid you though. As pieces of the old pie arise, you just look at them, and say, "Thanks but no thanks. I learned from that."

Then simply accept a new, better pie that actually tastes good. There are always points along the path that feel like a repeat, and this is simply because the old energy tries to follow you. If you look at it again and again, and keep going back to that mangled mess, again I stress, you will only add to that mangled mess some more. That is how you end up feeling so tangled up again and again in the gunk of the past. Look beyond that. We wish to give you an infusion of the future, but, even that sometimes can get you all mangled and gunked. If you are constantly thinking, "I will be better when this happens." Then you are simply living in the future, but things happen differently than you think.

Time is irrelevant when it comes to enjoying the journey. Even though most are focused so intently on time. If you look beyond time and more into different points in your life, you'll find things becoming easier to see and experience.

Prayer

Father,

Thank you for helping me not to look at the past and all the gunk back there. I will focus on what you have for me right here right now. Amen.

Chapter 13: Think New

Angel Kale

Move beyond the last failure. We know you often move into that same state of mind of, "This will fail too." We know it is very hard for you to overcome that last failure. The problem we see is, you put your attention and focus onto the failure again, even though this is a brand-new thing—if you so want it to be. The failure mindset will bring to you more things to see failure in again and again. This will only add to your surety that things are always failing for you. We want to help you see beyond that. It is not that you have failed, dear one, but you are just seeing the failure as you did before. You have chosen to see the failure instead of the victory from it.

Let me explain. Say you have missed something important, and you really do believe you failed at it thoroughly, but now you are looking for that same failure again in a new situation.

And if you look for it, it will show up. Your point of attraction is the focus of that thing that failed. You are calling to it and saying, "I am looking for you, please come to me!" It is a source of energy attraction, so of course it comes back and says, "Here I am!"

This is why it seems to fail, fail, fail at every turn. You are calling to it like a master calls his dog. It obeys and comes to you. If you treat each new thing, circumstance, or desire as fresh and new, and expect it to come the way a child would, then that thing you desire says, "Here I am!"

This is another thing we want to say too. If you see things as a failure, you will miss it entirely for what it is. It is a point of attraction you can learn from and say, "I don't want that." When you think that or feel that, you can then let it go, and focus in on what you do want. Such as a good-feeling relationship. But, you mustn't bring back your bad-feelings into your new relationship. For when you do that, the failure again says, "Here I am!" Do you see what we are saying here?

If you are going out and bringing light to people, and you are only dragging along the failure-mind, then you will only find that failure rears its head to you. If you go out with the mindset of greatness, of course, that is what will say, "Here I am!"

Think of it as you are the master, and it is your obedient, loving slave. It obeys on command. Whatever commands you give, those things will follow and obey you. What are you speaking, feeling, and expressing to your situations and relationships? They will answer with, "Here I am!" Every single time.

Prayer

Father,

Thank you for helping me focus on life, love, and success. I let go of the failure mindset, and I release and refresh myself to understand more. Amen.

Chapter 14: Gifts

Angel Mike

Of course you are now wondering more and more what your spiritual gift is, or how do you actually 'wake it up'. Perhaps you haven't seen any gift at all in yourself, and it makes you feel very inadequate about yourself. There are a few things I want to open up with you about those specific issues in your mind. First of all, you must understand that you all have a gift. It doesn't matter who you are, you carry a light, a flow, and a gift to help heal and restore this earth. Whether it be an act of kindness, or energy healing, or loving animals—those are all gifts that are important to the culture of this planet.

If you discount your gift, which to some of you seems so very tiny or small, you will pull out a thread in the woven tapestry of life. I'm sure some of you understand when one thread is pulled, how things can quickly unravel for others. This causes the beauty of the picture to be fragmented or distorted. We want to show you that you are just as valuable as those who you'd call, "In the public eye."

It takes determination to really know yourself. We say this very kindly, but many do not want to know themselves. Many of them tuck tail and run the other way! We are often puzzled by these actions, since we think you are all such beautiful, wonderful beings. Do not run from yourself, dear ones. This will only cause more confusion inside of you. One or two of you, or many more, often tell us, "I don't know how or what to do with my life." We know there are many things that are troubling. We also know that some of you are far more sensitive than others to that which is roving around you. To you we invite closer to our energy, because we know that it is very easy for you to slip into the other.

We will go into another thing for you. You are looking for more details when it comes to gifts, so we will help you with that. First of all, there is the gift of 'performance.' Now you are looking at me very oddly, because you often use that word in a different way than what we do. Performance is simply you are bringing out that which you practiced in life. So, if you are very well practiced as a public speaker, and you are inspiring to others, you are a performer to them.

This is not a negative word, it is a very well-thought of word to us. Because, we know that you have often practiced privately to help others heal. If you feel you are led to perform and be in front of the public eye, there is a few things you'll have to work on first. Most of it, we see, is practicing the art of performing to others. Many shy away from the public eye, and this is okay too, because they aren't gifted to stand before a crowd and speak or perform for them.

They have a different part which is neither better nor worse in our eyes. We know this is a different type of spiritual gift than most would speak to you, but we are okay with that. We also want to add, just because you are quiet, shy, or don't think you're good at performance that some of you are still gifted or pulled to do it. These are things you must overcome and practice in order to be able to get to that point. So, even if you are so called 'bad' at this gift, does not mean you cannot overcome the so called 'badness' of it. This is what we call practice makes perfect!

Another gift, we wish to bring to your attention is the gift of expectation. Now, you're really looking at me funny! The gift of expectation is a gift where you can go to others and help them expect the best of their life. This can be in the light of performance or not. We know there are many who are very good at expecting, despite the odds. We know there are those who will stand up against the dark waves and use the light to push it back. People call them lightworkers as well. They are those who share light, despite the darkness crowding around them. They cannot help but expect the positive light to come, because it is their gift, their core. You may wonder, why do we call it that? Why do we not just call it something else—but this is to help you understand in a very easy way.

Do you know someone who often times has their head in the clouds, or they seem to always bounce back after something has knocked them down? They will show you the silver lining, and sometimes we know it makes you annoyed or mad at them. This is because they are expecting the best!

There is also those we call "searchers", because they are searching out mysteries, and they also want to relay those mysteries to people in a positive way. Many times, the searchers are those who like the cracks, and often times shy away from the limelight, and don't want people to know their name. They still want to display their information, but they do so in a way that doesn't draw much attention to them. Sometimes those who are searchers do get discovered by the greater audience, and their message is spread far and wide. This is because the searcher has more gifts than just the searcher gift. Some just relay information, only to have someone else who is a performer take it and expand it into a broader view, and it becomes known to the masses.

The searchers are okay with this, because they feel their job is to simply search out truth and help for others. They are a beautiful gift that is highly needed to help bring energy of change to the world.

Prayer

Father,

Thank you for showing me my gift, and I can honor myself in it. Thank you for helping me look beyond the failures I've faced and truly focus in on what lays ahead of me. Amen.

Chapter 15: Awareness

Angel Gabriel

Living light lives inside of you. It is only a matter of understanding or bringing your conscious awareness into this state of being that you need. You are a spirit being, and everything is immediately available for you, but first you must become aware of these things. Don't fret or worry about the how it will happen, or what is needed. You will find things simply being there, because it is what you need.

The desire to move into your spiritual awakening, will also awaken what you need in order to open your eyes further. For example: the right materials will be placed in your hands in order to see clearer and clearer. Don't stress so much about the how, but rather focus on the wanting, but not in such a way that feels bad. Focus on the wanting in a way that feels liberating and good. You are an expression of love on this planet, and in that expression, there will be times you will not see yourself in the way you should.

This isn't because you are far off from your goal. This is simply because there is something trying to unfurl, and you must focus more and more onto it to see it unfurl further. There are buds that want to bloom inside of you. You must allow them to feel good, in order for them to fully unfold. That is how you'll see the fruition of them come to pass. If you think or say,

"Why is this not working like I wish it to?" And you are feeling bad about the unfolding of the bud on the inside, it will only cause more negative, not-good-enough feelings to manifest. If instead you see the bud, and your desire is to watch it unfold in a lovely way, you bring more energy to that wanting, and it speeds up the process very easily.

Prayer

Father,

Thank you for helping me focus in on the good-feelings around my desires. Help me keep my heart open and full of joy. Amen.

Chapter 16: Lighten Up

Angel Morgan

I had to throw a little humor in here. I mean you guys get far too serious about everything in life. You stress so hard about your gifts, abilities, or things happening around you. This isn't a matter of stressing, it's a matter of rejoicing! When you start coming to be who you were truly made to be, there is great happiness, joy, and laughter going on! It's like when a little kid does something for the first time. You celebrate! Even though they weren't perfect at it, you didn't care. You still threw a party, posted on Facebook, or texted everyone in the vicinity around you. You were happy! That is what we want you to focus on when it comes to your spiritual abilities. Celebrate every victory. It doesn't matter how tiny you think it is—celebrate it!

We are even suggesting taking yourself out, throwing a party, or writing yourself a note of appreciation. There are many times you make a step, and instead of going nuts with love about it, you heap criticism on yourself that it isn't enough. Or that you're not where you should be. That's just hogwash. Plain out hogwash. Would you speak that over a tiny child who made one step and fell? No! Of course not! You don't even care if they don't take another step. You still want everyone around you to be proud of that tiny accomplishment. This is how we want you to treat yourself with your spiritual gifts. I know it seems like it's taking forever. I see how you guys tap the watch, look at your phone, or scroll past. Many people need to take a little breather from 'time', and really, really let go into the now. If you really truly focus on the here and now, you'll see that you're much further than you ever imagined.

In fact, we want to challenge you with this. Keep a happy journal of all the little things you feel you're getting better at. Each day take an account, and if you ever feel as if those baby steps are not getting you anywhere, go back and look at that step-by-step journal of progress! Then throw a party about it! I hope you're getting this, I truly do. There is so much potential in you to run, play, and do amazing things.

Think about the greatest athletes in the entire world. They started off by taking one tiny step, wobbling, and falling on their butts, just like you! Here's the thing, they didn't get swayed by that tiny step. They knew that the more steps they took, the better they'd get. Look at those gifts for what they are, and appreciate yourself for them. If you look at others and you say, "But, look at how far they are. Or look at how much or many gifts they have." This will not aid you in your own discovery.

There is not better or worse, just different when it comes to spiritual gifts. We want to help shake you up from that mindset of him/her is better, better, better. When you start appreciating yourself for who you are, your gifts will shoot up beyond anything you could have imagined. This is going to be a fun ride. Just embrace it. Things will flow much smoother if you stop looking at all your teeny, tiny flaws constantly. That isn't helping anyone on this planet. Especially you! Think of it this way. If a baby is learning to walk, and you were constantly saying, "Oh, that's not how you do it. You aren't doing it right. You're wobbling too much." Get my point? If you were constantly critiquing the walking process, that baby would sit down and cry. Because, who wants to try to walk when they are getting criticized for their every step?

Now, look at yourself that way. Practice is a key component in this journey with your spiritual gifting. The more you practice it, the better you'll be. While practicing, don't beat yourself up about the 'oops and bloops' that happen along the way. Think of someone who is just learning to play an instrument.

Unless they are instantly gifted like some are, they have to go through the squeaks, mistakes, and other things in order to get to a pure, amazing sound. We know we are hammering this point, here, but it's something very important to see. We also want to stress to you that joy is important. Find things funny. Look at mistakes as something to grow by and just move on, man! There is no point in rehashing that stuff. It just adds negative fuel to the fire, and you don't want to spread that fire. Instead, feed the fire of your passion and watch it burn.

Prayer

Father,

Thank you for helping me celebrate every little step forward I make. I know you are helping, Father, to make those steps. Amen.

Chapter 17: Know thyself

Angel Kingsley

There is oft a time where I don't think people quite understand themselves. It's hard to understand your spiritual ability if you are questioning your own sense of self. If you feel you are 'confusing, unworthy, indecisive' for example, you will find it extremely hard to work with your gifting, and especially when working with others. If you cannot discern your own sense of self, you will struggle with discerning others as well. You may even find yourself throwing your own issues onto others as you practice with them, and this can make things very hard to understand and interpret. The way to be free of that, is to work on discovering the parts of yourself you run and hide from every day. If you feel things aren't working as they should, you must be quiet, and ask yourself what part of you is hiding and feeling ashamed of showing its face.

It sounds very disconnected, and that's because when you are disconnected from your own sense of self, it is very challenging to connect to others in a proper light. You may even find that it is challenging to understand your own moods and feelings, and that is why we are stressing to you to know yourself first. There can become such a need to help others, that you often times forget that you must help yourself first.

This is something we say, because we know a broken man cannot lift a broken man up and dust him off. A broken man must first ask for help and then after he is restored, help another broken man just like he was. Make sense? If you are striving to help others, but it is coming from a place of lack, we want to help you with that. We want to help you balance that. Needless to say, we are not expecting you to be 100% perfect inside. We know that is a journey all must face to continuously learn and grow in healing. What we are saying though is, know thyself first, and bring healing to thyself first. Afterward, you will find the joy and strength to lift others as well.

Brokenness cannot restore brokenness. Just like a wounded man cannot heal a wounded man. It is simply not within them. They must first find wholeness in their wound, and then reach out to the wounded after. Yes, we are saying reach out still, because we also know that in a state of woundedness there must sometimes be a hand to show the way. You can become that hand, and we also know though, that the healing isn't on your shoulders, but the one who needs to open up and receive the healing. Don't stress about healing others. You don't do a thing. You simply remind them, or show them the healing process, and they reach out for themselves and grasp a hold of it. It just takes a nudge sometimes for others to truly get to that point. Make sense?

Prayer

Father,

Thank you for helping me heal. I want to reach others too, and I know that bringing healing to my own self will help me get to the place I need to go. Amen.

Chapter 18: True Nature

Angel Mallory

There are many who feel as if they have delusions or are deluded in their path. That can be a crying shame, because they shut down the things that are trying to develop inside of them. They call it 'weird, crazy, or stupid' and can't seem to grasp that those things could be the beginning stages of a gift. There are times when people don't see themselves for what they truly are—a divine being of light, love, and joy.

You were put here for a divine purpose—to love and be loved. You are ever growing and changing in this life, and we want you to know we will help you toward the next level of growth you are trying to achieve. There are things that feel out of alignment, and inside of you it feels bad. That is because your true inner spirit, and the thoughts or things you are feeling, are contradicting themselves, so you feel the negative results from it.

Misalignment is the greatest form of pain for most, because it is like trying to force something together that is not a match, and in doing so, it causes friction and pain. Think of a relationship you've had where there is only friction and tension between the both of you. This is because your thoughts, feelings, and desires are not aligning properly. This does not mean they cannot align properly with understanding and love. This just means at the current state you're in, things are out of alignment. If you refocus on what you so desire, and you both come to the place of understanding one another through love and communication, you can realign and live in a peaceful, aligned place. This is how we view most things. If you are feeling discontent about your gift, and you are frustrated at the lack of it, we ask you first to ask yourself if you feel misaligned with your gifting. Do you feel as if it is doing one thing, while you are doing another? Do you see yourself how we see you?

These are just small tips to help you realign with your true source of love. Once you start recognizing when you are misaligned, you can carefully and with love, realign with your true source of love. Once you do that, your gift will feel effortless and easy to flow in. That is how it always should work. See, we all want you to come to the place where you feel your gift supplies for you as well as for others.

If you feel others just 'take, take, take' your energy from your gift, it can become very frustrating for you, and indeed you'll stop wanting to give to others all together. You must take time to give to your own self before launching into a career where you simply give, give, give. This is for your own safety and energy's sake. If you cannot seem to find that space of healing in yourself, you will find it very difficult to give healing to others too.

We also wish to point this out to you. If you are giving out of a place of lack energy, you will only receive that which you give out. You must first find the true source of peace, love, and abundance on the inside of you, so that you can give out of that place instead. We also want to say this to you. When you give to others, you are simply awakening them to their true source of love and energy, so that they can learn to tap into their flow as you do.

Now, this seems like, "Then I would run out of those to help if I did that." No, we say. You will never, ever run out. For there are so many who do not yet understand, nor are they at the place or ability to really grasp that which you're helping them achieve. They will need much from you, but you must first ask yourself, "Am I giving to me? Am I filling me?"

For if you try to give from the place of lack, you will not feel full. You will feel their need and their desperation instead, because it mirrors your own lack inside. See what I'm saying with this? First fill YOU. Then help others, and show them the way to their own source inside. Empower them to see who they truly are.

Prayer

Father,

Thank you for helping me fill myself first, so that I don't mirror lack in other people. Thank you for showing me how to help others get to their own source of love and connection. Amen.

.

Chapter 19: Be In-tune

Angel Kale

Principles build one day at a time, so don't feel as if you have to rush into something with full speed ahead. That can be very, very tiring indeed. If you are pushing yourself, beyond your own limits, you will only run yourself down into the ground when you go to use your spiritual gifts. Be spiritually in-tune with your own needs, and you'll find things working for you. If you are trying to push too hard and too fast, you may find that you throw in the towel quickly. You'll not understand how it works properly. If you find you are in-tune, and it seems very overwhelming far too much, you can ask for things to slow down. You can adjust how quickly things come or don't come, according to your own desire.

It may seem like you don't have control over the onslaught of information or feelings that are hitting you, but you do. You must know that you are the creator of this reality, so if you feel as if your gift is overpowering you, then you are allowing it to have that overpowering role in your life. There is balance with spiritual gifts. There is timing. If you feel as if the timing is stressful or is causing more pain than good, you can ask for things to process slower. There is no wrong or right way to use a spiritual gift. It simply takes knowing and practice. Many of you are fearful.

This is the line of thought we want to help you get to. Because, you can access your own line of thought, and heal, help, and bring joy, but you also can bring an understanding only through your own limitations of those thoughts. Or, you can access a greater thought, and that is far above your own or the other person's. This takes persistence and time, and of course a deep love, trust, and understanding.

There is a flow, you can tap into, but you must be willing to go beyond your own natural line of thought. This can be a very unknown and scary territory for those practicing their gifts. You must get over the fear of failure, or the fear of not understanding to access this type of thought process. Don't worry about the ups and downs or the mishaps that seem to happen. If you are afraid of mistakes, that will be all you attract into your reality. You'll see mistakes at every corner all the time. So, make sure you become aware of these things, and reach above into the higher realms with us.

Prayer

Father,

Thank you for helping me access your love and thoughts toward people. I want to be aware of my own line of thinking verses your thoughts for others, Father. Amen.

Chapter 20: Colors

Angel Raziel

Colors can be very helpful for you. You're probably wondering what in the world I'm talking about, but let me show you. There are influences all around you in the forms of energies. Colors are also an influence on your natural mind. It can bring clarity or confusion. If you feel you are drawn to a color, this is because it's energy is speaking to you at the moment. If you feel a color rejuvenates you, that is because the energy is again speaking to you. Wear the colors you feel best in. Have the colors around you that brings joy to your mind. Especially when you are bringing your gift to the light. The more color you access around you, the better the gift will flow.

A colorful routine will also help you access places in your mind that have been dormant. What do I mean by that? Let me show you. First of all, say you feel you best hear, feel, know, and access your gift by a certain way. Such as: soft music, candlelight, smells, stones, or colors around you. These little rituals can become very healing and energizing to you. When you do them, your spirit knows 'it is time to access my information', and this becomes very grounded in you. That is what I am wanting to point out to you. Colors can be part of the routine. There are many pinpoints of awareness that can help access your gift in a stronger way. Find the smells that attract you. Find the colors.

Find the sounds. Those that bring you a feeling of joyful expectation, will bring you into a further awareness of your gifting. Don't be shy with the rituals that draw you deeper and closer.

Prayer

Father,

Thank you for showing me and helping me access that which draws me into my awareness of my gift. Amen.

Chapter 21: Teamwork

Angel Lance

Teamwork. That is something we want to bring to your attention right now. When you join up with those who can help you, aid you, and show you how to connect divinely to your truest you, then you'll not only be able to discover your spiritual gifts quicker, you'll find great joy in doing them with others. There is no man unto himself, even if it feels that way at times. Everyone has uncovered feelings in themselves of inadequacies, and they all must move past them in order to be their authentic version of who they are.

You can know others have been there before you. They can give you encouragement to remind you that you also can receive and open up to the degree you want to. There are those who have learned the hard way, and those who have learned the way they followed. Some cannot help but follow the beaten, traveled path of those before them, such as in a mother or father figure. It is preprogrammed within their consciousness and unconsciousness. It starts to formulate all on its own. Don't associate with those who make your inner being feel bad or inadequate all the time. What we mean by that is, if you feel like others are constantly putting you down or shaming you into your proper *place,* then that is not the company you will want to keep. It is quite different however if you are the one shaming yourself in the company of those who seem like they have it altogether or are functioning more thoroughly in the gifting they have.

This can simply be a mirror for you to look at in yourself. If you feel as if you won't arrive, such as they are, you must ask yourself why you are doubting your own self. Why are you feeling that jealousy or inadequacies arising? Jealousy can be the number one killer of awakening a gift. This is simply because as the little bud is beginning to poke through the earth, jealousy tries to make it grow faster and pulls on its roots to grow before its timing. This can cause many bitterness-type feelings. Look at it this way even. Say you have a deep desire to have something—whatever it may be, and it seems that the thing you desire keeps popping up but in other people's lives. How do you react? Do you feel as if that means it is getting ten steps closer to you? Or does it feel as if you are getting ten steps behind? This determines the manifestation of your desire.

It may feel hard to not feel bad or jealous when things constantly pop up around you, but I want to advise you to watch those beliefs and feelings. For if you feel bad, when others feel good, you will only attract more of the sad, bad feelings, and you will only see it more and more. Instead, look at the energy surrounding you as in, "This is getting closer to me!" Then you will have a shift in perspective altogether, and it will help the energy you desire to manifest in a quicker, much lighter way.

Prayer

Father,

Thank you for helping me remain joyful even when others get what I really desire. I can remain positive knowing that the thing I desire is ten steps closer to me! Amen.

Chapter 22: Magnet

Angel Jaziel

There is a direction I want to take you with these words. Follow closely to them, and you'll start to hear, see, and feel what I am talking about. There is a magnet inside of you that has been there for as long as you have been alive. You are a complete source of magnet energy, and you can learn to expand it, if you so desire. Which I have a feeling you want to do that! So, if you can listen carefully, you'll feel your energy already growing and expanding. Do you know how some people say, "Expand your mind?" That is kind of the premise of what I want to talk about in this section here.

Expanding your mind takes choice and action. It also takes allowing too. For example, if you were taught that a table was only 4x4, and every table you owned was that dimension, it may be very hard for you if someone said, "I have a 9x9 table." You would think it very strange they'd say that to you, because all you've ever seen or known is a 4x4.

Here's something we want you to consider though. If you went to that friend's house who had a 9x9 table, and you physically sat down and measured it, your thinking would expand, correct? You couldn't deny that the table was much bigger than you ever thought a table could be. This is a lot of how a spiritual gifting works. Many people are very afraid to even believe there is a much bigger table out there, and they are unwilling to attempt to believe it. Then some of them stumble across a person who is attempting to expand their thinking mind to believe in much bigger tables, and there is a resistance to it. Some of it is because that type of thinking is "wrong, unrealistic, or not solid", and they shut down the expansion before it can even take root. Then they may run across one who has proven, by a point of attraction, that those things they are saying are indeed *solid forms*, and now the person is faced with a choice.

Of course, there will always be those who cannot expand, even when they see the proven 9x9 table, and they will stay in denial of a greater, larger, expanded view, and they will not listen. These types do not worry about so much, for they are too afraid to let go of their 4x4 views of life. Even if you tell them that things can fit much better with this expanded view; they will deny it. So, shrug off those types of encounters, for they will only wear you out trying to force or explain your 9x9 view. This is a waste of your time, effort, or energy.

If you encounter instead a person who says, "Can I see your 9x9 table?" Then you know that they are ready to expand past their old point of view. You can never force people to apply the things you've applied. You must only invite them to apply the view themselves. This is how we want you to view your gifts, and also the gifts of others. There will always be those who doubt your abilities to achieve that which you desire, or your abilities to point them to the bigger view, but you must just allow them to stay in their very limited view of creation.

Prayer

Father,

Thank you for helping me with my point of view. I want to expand my thinking and reach others. I desire to help them also see this bigger, broader point of view. Amen.

Chapter 23: Practice

Angel Kale

It's time to get to work now. You're probably wondering what I mean by that. Let me go into a bit of detail about it for you. There is of course an awakening, spiritual process, but there is also a season of working with what you've learned in life. If you have learned that you are intuitive, for example, you must give place to practice that which you've learned. You will pick up more, the more you practice. Just like you practice anything else in life, your gifts will get stronger and more fine-tuned with practice and time.

Don't give up before you finetune that gift! You'll need a few things in order to practice what you're desiring: a willing partner and a belief that you are learning and growing each time you practice. Stretch yourself—and perhaps have a partner you don't know very well. Don't use your best friend, but ask someone you feel slightly comfortable with still. At least while you are in the practicing stages.

Most people are very intimidated to attempt a new thing or to even try to stretch that which they have. Sometimes when you use a muscle, for example, it aches or hurts afterward. Well, this can be the same as for intuitive gifts as well. You may have a bump, a bruise, or a few oops along the way, but you mustn't beat yourself up about those bruises or cuts, just keep practicing! You'll get to where you need to go eventually, and then you'll look back and be happy you kept moving past the potholes that you bumped into. It'll work out for your highest good, if you so believe that way.

Prayer

Father,

Thank you for helping me finetune my gift. Help me find the right people to practice on. I really appreciate your help. Amen.

Chapter 24: Talk to yourself

Angel Mallory

There must first be a few discussions you make with yourself before you 'get out there'. These discussions can be a bit of work for you. Don't think of it as an exhausting, never ending thing, but a thing you must work through if you want to see yourself really get polished and much more confident. The first discussion with yourself is this: I am not perfect, and it's okay that I make some mistakes. When you understand that, you pull the pressure off yourself, and you start allowing yourself to breathe and be human. Don't expect 100% accuracy with everything you do while tuning up your gift. Expect some things to be crazy or off when you practice. It's okay. Don't lose confidence when you do so. That is the first pep talk you'll want to give yourself. Look yourself in the eye and say, "I love you, even when you make an oops. It's okay."

The second thing you'll want to discuss with yourself is your ability to hear, feel, see, and smell. These are very natural for you in your physical form, and you don't struggle to believe that they are working in proper order. Well, same is true of your spiritual senses. You need to be aware that they also operate on a higher frequency with you. If you feel that one is blocked, that may be the case, but it is just as easy to unblock those senses fully. The more you are aware of those senses in operation, the more you'll be able to tune into them very easy. It's like a tuning fork, once you tune into it, you'll pick up the same frequency quicker. Look at your spiritual senses much the same way you look at your natural senses. Natural. Normal. Easy. Like breathing. It shouldn't be a struggle to open those other senses. It's a matter of trust and belief that they are actually in operation. Such as this: ask your spiritual eyes to open and look at a situation for you. Write down what you see. Or ask your spiritual ears to open and ask them what they hear. Write down what you hear. This is a process, but the more you get in-tune with the spiritual senses you have, you will notice that some take more prominence than others.

This is not to say the others are out of tune or not working—it is quite like how some have a better ability to dribble a basketball, while another has the gift of painting or singing. It is just a different one that is more attuned or stronger. It doesn't mean an artist couldn't learn to carry a tune, but it would take much more work for them if they aren't what most people call "a natural" at that particular gift.

You must first identify within yourself what you feel is inside of you. Do you often sense what will happen? Or do you hear a voice speaking to you? Do you see something in pictures, words, or colors that come true? Do you often times have body feelings that go through you when you are around people? These are all different gifts you can tune into.

Here is something we must stress with you very carefully. When you see somebody with a natural ability such as they are heightened with sight, sense, or hearing, and you feel you don't have anything that just comes easily to you, don't despair. Don't look at them and feel frustrated that you don't have that. Just know that you too can operate in your gift with time, love, patience, and practice. For just as in the physical world how there are some that have a very natural gift, there are some in the non-physical realm who also appear that way too. It doesn't mean you cannot attune your gift as well.

You may find that you are naturally attracted to a specific gift—or you find yourself reading materials on that gifting. This is the beginning stages of your awakening. Allow it to happen. Breathe in the newness of your gift. You will find teachers, helpers, and materials that draw you. Go to them. If you are pouting and saying, "I don't know what my gift is!", I want you to start listening to what's going on in the inside of you. Are you feeling drawn to a certain book, teacher, or videos? If so, read, listen, and watch! This is how you start to shake off the old and awaken the newness inside of you. If you have laid asleep for years, when you awaken, there are new sights, sounds, smells, and touch. Just as a newborn baby is in awe of its brand-new world, so also be in awe of your brand-new world.

Prayer

Father,

Thank you for helping me find my spiritual gift and practice in it. Thank you for drawing me to the right materials I need to awaken my gifting. Amen.

Chapter 25: Growth

Angel Mallory

Destiny is calling you, but it's up to you to listen to her insistent calling. Many times, those who long to awaken, are ignoring the feelings or sensations that have been going on for quite some time. They are struggling with the growth end of it, and many want to remain as they are and still receive the spiritual gift. This is not the case. Whenever a new gifting is coming to fruition, it brings forth new tests and lessons in order to fully come to pass. Many times, those who are in the biggest battles of their life, come out with the strongest gifts. Why is that? Because they learned that they had to trust what was happening in the middle of the mess. They also will grow the most in that period—if they so choose to.

Most of you, when you are struggling, start reaching for materials that will better your life. Books, videos, clips, art, or people you can learn from. You want to grow. You want to change, because where you're at, it hurts to stay the same. This is called—awakening. Welcome it. It isn't an easy path when you are being shaken from your deep slumber on this planet and brought before this mountain you must overcome. Look at all the great teachers, and you will find a very similar story. They overcame obstacles, and through it they grew into the teachers they are now. That is why when you are attracted to a certain teacher, it is because their struggle and their lesson is drawing you. What they overcame now becomes your information. If you allow your own struggles and lessons to help you grow, you will also turn around and teach another through their hard times. This is the human process. Pain equals growth. We don't want you to be afraid of the growth process, and the progression that is happening within and around you, but we also want to be real and tell you there is pain involved with growth. Why else would you be reaching for a teacher? You are uncomfortable with the knowledge you are at and wish to enhance yourself.

Some of the greatest ideas have been birthed out of pain—or a state of discontent. Those who refuse to settle into the norm, they are the ones who make a strong mark on this earth. Many people pick up where that teacher left off and create an even greater, expanded version of their lesson. Wake up, darlings, but also know that the lesson you are going through right now will be your greatest tool when you go through it. Learn from it. Grow. Expand.

Prayer

Father,

Thank you for helping me grow, learn, and expand as I go through this tough lesson. I choose to take my pain, learn from it, and grow into a teacher myself to help others. Amen.

Chapter 26: Health

Angel Hannah

We want to talk to you a little bit about health. For this is a subject that many people glaze over, and it has a big part of awakening your spiritual gift. If you find you are drawn to a certain thing again and again, but you are ignoring the impulse, and instead eating that which you find "comforting" or "easy", this will only hinder your spiritual access and growth. For example: if you keep feeling drawn to sugary foods, this is not from the awakening process, but an addiction to an old process. They become habits. It becomes far too easy to ignore the little signs we are sending you to improve your physical body. If you keep hearing, seeing, and feeling signs such as: go outside, buy this plant, eat this type of food, then those are signs to help you grow. If you continue to ignore them, you'll find yourself growing weary or hindered on your path.

This isn't something most people want to hear, and unfortunately, it's because they have a habit of eating the wrong sugar, starchy, or otherwise habitual foods on a daily basis. They don't want anyone to make them give up those things, so they harbor or hide it away. What I am saying isn't to make you feel bad or take away your favorite snack, but rather to help you awaken and grow into the real, authentic version of yourself. You will feel there is things calling you to them, and you must allow them access in order to find more enjoyment out of them. Have you ever noticed you used to be drawn to a certain thing, but after you improved, say your emotional or mental health, that certain food no longer had any appeal? That is because the mental and emotional states are tied to the foods you consume. Of course, there is much research with foods and how they affect you spiritually and physically, and we will not touch on that much here in this. We just want to stress to you that if you are drawn to a particular food, which is healthy for you, make sure you be agreeable with it.

Prayer

Father,

Thank you for showing me the right food to buy and eat to keep myself healthy. Amen.

Chapter 27: More

Angel Lance

There is always more. That is something we want to stress to you when it feels like you've topped out, or things are stagnant concerning your gifting. If it feels you've hit that brick wall, it is simply time to expand and grow again. Which we know sometimes those seasons of stagnation can be extremely wearying and frustrating for you. Don't worry. We are going to help you grow and expand even more. Open up your mind, and allow things to start stimulating again. Don't be afraid to see things from different views or points.

Learning to expand is a process. Learning to allow yourself to expand is also a process. There are many of you who have put up boundaries on your expansion, and this is mostly out of fear of what is "out there". It became a stagnant point in your life because of it. It also can seem there are many, many, many of the same, but we want to stress this is not the case. For all teachers and healers have a different way in which they operate with their gifting. This will be true even for you. We do stress that you go to those teachers which you are drawn to, but we also stress to allow yourself to open up more and try new things. Do things your way as well.

The flow will feel different for all. The key is not to stress about the direction of the flow. Just allow it to actually open and flow. There will be a catapulting of your gift when you open and receive. In fact, it may even feel as if you are tripping because you are running so quickly forward. You'll want to absorb many things, and this is good, but also be aware that the more you absorb, the more you'll need a form of releasing the built-up energy that is coming your way.

Prayer

Father,

Thank you for helping me expand and open up even more. Help me know where to release that which I have on the inside of me. Amen.

Chapter 28: Tune Up

Angel Jamel

We are setting up a channel with you at the moment, and we want you to tune into that channel. There are many of you who are simply not attuned to the right station, and we are trying our best to get you to the right place, so you can hear, feel, and know what is happening around you. Some of you get pieces of information that bleed through, but they still feel very unclear, and we know you want much more fine tuning with it all. We want to open up the doorway for you, and it is simply a matter of shifting some of your awareness or focus on the subjects at hand.

First of all, stop focusing on the nots. For example: I don't have this ability. I struggle with this. I'm too scared. All of these are nots. We say the word nots, and we think of them as truly *knots.* Because they tangle you up in their energy, and it seems you can't find your access out of these crazy situations that tie you up. It is a giant loop you go through, until you finally cry out for help. We want to help you access this new way of thinking, but you must be ready and willing to let go of all those nots. *You can* is a much better thing to hang onto. The focus shift is very important, because until you shift that point of focus, you will only get more of the same nots. It will be an endless frustration for you in each day.

The root cause of most or dare we say *all* of your problems is the focusing in on the nots, instead of the haves. When you look at life for what you have, a shift and point of attraction begins to happen. Once you see what you have, the point of attraction says, "Yes sir! Yes, miss! I will give you more of that!" It doesn't fuss around and say, "She probably meant this instead of that. Or he probably didn't really want that." That is not how it works. It just comes according to your focus or point of attraction.

There is what we call a tipping point. This tiny little point is a focus you put all your energy and attention on, and many times, it's something you don't really want! What ends up happening is you push and push against that thing, until that thing falls over and makes a mess on the floor! Then you say, "I didn't want that!" But, the point of attraction says, "Yes, you did. It's all you thought about every day. I was obeying and gave it to you."

This is how it works, dears. You must not focus in on the tipping point or that which you do not want so much. I hear you say, "But, it's so hard not to focus on the nots. I can't seem to get myself to focus on the haves in my life." To this we say, "It is much easier if you stop the stories you tell yourself. You must first learn what stories are going around and around in there. For some of them are very sneaky in the way they do things." That is the first step to finding out where your tipping point is. And, we say tipping point can also be a good, good thing. You can have this focused attention on what you have, and the tipping point says. "Look, they want that!" And bonk, it tips over, and you see the manifestation of it. Then you rejoice and get really happy, because more of what you desire came to you. Learn to recognize those tipping points, and allow them to shift into the energy you so desire for your life.

If you are wanting more of a joyfulness in your life, instead of focusing in on *when I have this I will have that*. Focus in on, *I have joyfulness now*. When things become your joy, it is very hard for us to not tell you, "That is not how you work it." But, when you look beyond the thing, and into the feeling of joyfulness, that is when the thing shows up! Make sense to you? Joyfulness isn't a matter of *stuff* it is a matter of *you*. You. You. You. We say this quite fiercely, even if trying to make you smile a bit with it too. You are a point of joyfulness. When you go within and find the joyfulness, it can't help but bring you the things you so want and desire. They become something your inner being says, "I deserve this. I love this. This feels good."

As you are feeling good inwardly, the outward responds with, "yes sir, yes miss!" It cannot but help come to you as it should.

Prayer

Father,

Thank you for helping me feel good. You love to bring me the things I desire. Thank you for all I have, and I know more is coming to me. Amen.

Chapter 29: Create

Angel Kale

Little bits seem to happen for you quite often, but it doesn't seem like enough to really feel satisfying. Your gift is trying to awaken, and you feel like it's slow or you're doing something to hinder it from blooming much faster. Resistance happens. We're here to help you stop resisting everything that we are trying to bring along your path. When you get into the state of allowing, there will be a much clearer path before you. In fact, your thought process will be much easier and faster than ever before.

You sometimes look at others and you covet or desire what they have, and this only brings you more to covet or desire that others have. Instead, look at what they have and reflect on it, and say, "I am able to have that too. We all have plenty." This puts you into a better frame of mind of receiving from what you are putting outward. We know you are wondering, "But, what about my abilities? How do I make them better? How do I even know what they are?" We see the stress on your face, and we know you are trying to awaken. Instead, we will challenge you with this. Allow it to awaken. Each morning, wake up with a smile on your face and think, "Today I am awakening even more. Today I am practicing and learning my spiritual gift even more."

Do not resist it. If you feel bad or as if it doesn't work for you then you will only draw more of those feelings to you about your spiritual gift. We know this often times feels like make-believe, but if you truly look into the heart and mind of an artist who creates, you'll see that it started off as a make-believe image in their mind. That is how all things are created. First a belief, then a creation. This is how we want you to view everything. Once you see it, feel it, and know it, it has to show up for you. If you picture yourself as a powerful creator of your reality, that is exactly what you'll become.

Prayer

Father,

Thank you for creating me to be a powerful creator. You have given me an amazing gift, and I want to use it every day to help better myself and this world. Amen.

Chapter 30: Simple Belief

Angel Malachi

We want to finish off this book with a bang! I think you are starting to grasp what we are talking about, but we want to make sure it's really ingrained in your head by now. The keys to awakening are quite simple. Belief. Trust. Love. Patience. Of course many more things than these, but we know you will get there as you walk it out. There is a time and a period of what we simply call: practice. You must take the time consciously and practice. Practice on yourself. Practice on others.

Don't be afraid to stretch the muscles of your spiritual gift, and as you do this, you'll gain more practice and even more opportunities to grow. There is always growth when it comes to awakening. For if we threw it all on you at one time, your physical body would not be able to handle the amount of energy flow that it takes to handle what we'd call more "practiced gifts".

For you often times look at those who have it all together, and you think, "I want to be like that." But, you don't always see the path they took to receive that revealed gift. For all of you have the gifts, it just takes time to unveil them to your physical reality. Are you willing to walk the shoes of those who have much more practiced gifts? Are you willing to follow along beside us, and we will help you uncover it? For if you feel the strain or the uncomfortable feelings of growth and practice, we know sometimes you want to run the other way! We are not saying awakening is so very horrible, and some people will say it is, but we will say that it is a stretching and a growing. Some do not like that period of time until they later reflect and say, "Yes, it was such a crazy time! But, look at where I am now!"

Most of you only see the aftermath of those who have been stretched, poked, and prodded into who they are today. You don't always see the tears, fears, worries, and many nights of practicing their gifting to feel better in themselves. The inner practice takes effort and time, but we do not want you to feel discouraged about these times of growth. We want you to look forward to those times of stretching and pain, and understand that those times are simply good times to learn and grow even more.

How does one learn a new skill in general? Be it fixing something or desiring to do something better with your life? You read, learn, watch, and hear what you want to do. So, yes it takes some time and practice, but in the end, you can do this amazing thing you could never do before. We know sometimes you want to give up before you started, and this comes from a root case inside of you as a child. There are many of you who don't even understand why everything just feels hard, and this is because you were fed a mindset about it as a child. That life is hard. Those words are something many adults say to children when they don't know what to say to a problem. Instead of telling the children, "We create what we believe." They just simply say, "Life is hard." So, children believe everything has to be hard in their reality. Do you see how this has become a problem in the world? If everyone around you thinks life is hard, that is all they will simply create. Hard. Hard. Hard. It will be as if all they see is problems—and you understand what I am saying, because you understand how you do it to yourself! You see life as having hurdles and mountains, and it is very tiring to climb this or beat this back. What if you simply started saying, "I live life with ease. Things come to me that I desire." Then you'd see life in a very new light.

Have you also met children that what they desire just seems to appear? We call this child-like faith, or the faith of a child. Many of you look at those children and think, "Why do they have it so easy, and I have to stress and strain all the time with my desires?" Is it simply because you have forgotten that your natural state of being is to just have life be easy and flow with you? As you grew up, did you lose that simple desire that it would happen for you, because you were so very deserving of the thing you wanted?

Many of you were taught, as you grew, if one thing didn't happen you desired and it seemed to be taking much longer than you wanted, that life is *hard*. Your child-like minds sucked in the knowledge that there must be a time after a while where life gets harder, and now you can no longer just create that easy reality. Remember how your parents said to you, "Your prayers seem to be answered so quickly!" And you were happy, because you knew it was true! Then, for some reason, when something seemed too slow, they said, "Ah, we don't always get what we want. Life can be hard." Now your sponge-like child mind said, "They know because they are truth to me."

Parents start to teach their children the way life is, instead of the way the child can create their life! This is unfortunate, because children have a purer desire and stronger faith of creating ability than adults. It is not because the adults cannot create their own reality, in fact they do every day by focusing on what they do not want! Children have an unwavering knowing that it will come.

As children, they are handed things without them striving and working for that thing they desire. As they grow, they simply get fed that things aren't that way. They get told that now they have to 'work' for those things they once got handed to them so easily. It shifts their point of attraction into working, working, working. Then they grow frustrated with the working, and they think, "How did I have it so easy as a kid? How did I just have those things I desired?" And then they think, "It must be because kids are just like that. They get what they pray or desire."

This is the way it seems to be. What people don't understand though is that they can still have a child-like faith, and be unwavering in it, and still draw to them what they need and desire. You must go beyond your reality and into the thing you are searching for. This takes practice to understand, but you will get there! We know you will see it very clearly and very soon. You'll start to pinpoint those things you attract already. This is a huge part of your awakening, and we want you to see that.

For example: if you, as a child, felt you had a natural, easy-flowing gift, and things just simply came to you out of the blue, you can understand that your gift did not die or leave. It simply got overridden by your adult-fed brain that things start to get hard for you. *No, no, no.* Things didn't get hard, you just started focusing on the difficulties of the adult world around you. A child-like world is very easy and playful. Joyful. Children live for one thing—joy. They want to find the fun in life, and they uncover it every single day. This is what we want to bring you back around to.

It is not to ignore the lessons you learned as you grew, but to look at the state of mind your child-like heart was in. It believed. It trusted. It simply asked and knew it would come to pass. This is the state we want to help you achieve again. There is much beauty in a child-like mind. We simply say this to you; have the child-like faith as before. We know you can find that child inside of you who once simply believed and had it happen. There are some things you see as such a big deal, or a big problem, you think, *that is far too big to handle for a child!* But, that is where we want to help you with that. Children don't strive. Children don't make things happen or force it to. They just believe it. Then it happens.

Take for example, their dinners. You, as the adult, know you are the creator of their dinner, but a child just knows *food will be there*, and food is there. You are part of their beliefs and creations for their life.

We want to direct you to that in yourself. People may be the ones giving you those desires you so want, but your belief is what is drawing them to you.

We know you are wondering why we are talking about this in a book about awakening spiritual gifts, but we want you to grasp the reality of this child-like faith. For a child believes they are special, up until someone instills in them they are not. When you let go of the words of others, or the failures you feel have happened, you'll begin to recognize the child-like, unwavering faith you truly have. You can grasp that you are special again. We use that word lightly, because we know special seems very funny sounding at times to you. But, we also want to stress it. Because, a special person, is someone who has abilities and potential. You are that person who has many things to add to the world around you. If you so believe. You'll attract those who you will help, and who will also help you.

You can look at the lessons of life as that— lessons. The battles, the hills, and the mountains are directing you back to your roots. Your child-like heart. Your child-like faith to believe that you are truly special. Don't give into the adult-minded version where it keeps feeding you, "Life is hard. Life is hard." Those words are not even your true nature. Your true nature just allowed things to fall into place. You didn't worry about your next meal or how you'd get things. As children, you just requested, expected, and received. Maybe you are thinking, *I never had that as a child.* This is because the adults in your life over road that natural ability to create, and they fed you the *Life is Hard* mantra since you were very small. We know that is the case with some of you, and we apologize for those adults, because they also were fed that same mantra from the adults in their life. It is something passed down from adult to adult. They have a hard time reversing it toward their children.

Reach beyond to the child-like heart within, and find that it is easy to create. It is easy to receive. Don't worry about the how or where it'll come from in your life. Just understand it will come. This is key to understanding your own spiritual awakening. You may not know how you will get the knowledge or understanding, but you can grasp that it will come. You will feel pulled or drawn to things, and that is where you should go. You were drawn to these words, and so they are boosting and helping you get you to where you need to go. There is no accident you were drawn to this book or these words. You were drawn here by your inner creating ability. You are also understanding more now, because you were meant to read these words and follow them.

Make sense to you? We know all of this can seem very curious or confusing at times. We know you have to bite off a little bit at a time. It's time to grasp that your mind is much larger and bigger than society has fed to you. It can hold an endless amount of storage, and you can grasp that you are creating even when your consciousness is very confused. The powerful being within you grasps much deeper.

Say this to yourself as well, "I am a powerful creator of my reality. I am a powerful creator of my spiritual gift. I choose to awaken it." When you make powerful statements to yourself, those powerful statements begin a forward motion. Then you may wonder why you feel drawn to certain things. This is your powerful statement in play. Allow it to unfold. Rather like a countdown calendar, where you unfold each day to see what it brings. Make joyful living an intention, and you'll discover each day brings a new clear understanding and direction.

This makes life much more adventurous instead of dreading what the day will bring. Or expecting things to be *hard* as we have stressed several times. Instead, expect good, good things are in process. These things are guaranteed to come, because it is the natural way life is. Life is naturally easy. Life comes with ease. Life flows the direction you create it to flow. You are a powerful creator. You are a powerful healer. Your natural state of being is healed, loved, healthy, and whole. Your natural state of being is flowing with ease. It is only because you were taught discontent, resistance, and frustration that you are feeling that way. You learned those things by the others around you. Your natural state is trust and ease. Does this make sense for you?

We want you to know that your awakening can come with ease. Yes, we did say there is pain sometimes, and we know this sounds as if it is contradicting, and we say it can bring pain only because of the transition from the adult-like mind to the child-like mind again. You may have to put up with a few bumps to get you to that place, but once you grasp the meaning of what we are saying, you will find it quite easy. You will understand the meaning of all of this when you finally reach the other end.

Flow into your gifting. Be at ease. Be child-like.

Prayer

Father,

Thank you for helping me think like a child again. I desire a child-like faith, and I know you are helping me go back to that. Amen.

Chapter 31: Spiritual Understanding

Angel Kafe

We wanted to add one or two more things to help you on your path to spiritual awakening. It is often a path where people feel great pain, instead of what we'd love you to feel which is joy. The joy is what helps you move forward into the next stage of spiritual awakening. If you feel a dread, an obligation, or a sense of unhappiness, you must see what you are following and why? Are you doing this path for yourself or others? Were you raised to put others first, and in doing so completely neglected your own sense of self?

If this is ringing true to you, I wish to help you with that journey. The path of joy is one of least resistance. It is the one that lights you up, makes you feel alive, and you are excited to walk it out. This is the path we wish to show you. This is the path that you will find your greatest wishes and desires coming to pass. There is a belief, we know you have sometimes, that is to neglect thyself because it is deemed holy or righteous. Where we want to stress the opposite. Bring joy to yourself, and you will find your path easy.

Caring for others will come from the place of love and happiness—instead of regret and fearfulness. The fearfulness that others won't like you, accept you, or help you, can lead you to a very stunted life. Find the wings to fly and fly! Don't let others drag you into their system of beliefs. We know that you question your own beliefs quite a lot, and you wonder if you are just out there weird or strange, but we want to show you that your path is always going to be different than another. There are no two paths that are equal. For that is what you've been sent here to do. Find the path of least resistance, and find joy in that path!

As you awaken to that path, you'll find it becomes easier and easier to follow your joy or your bliss as some call it. Because, when you wake up and feel good, you will expect good, and you will live in good. You will find more and more good to talk about, love, and enjoy. The joyfulness of your life will draw others, and you can show them how to tap into their own source of joy too. This is where we want to take you on this journey of awakening your spiritual gifts. This is what we desire for you greatly.

Bring yourself up to a higher level of consciousness, and that is where you will find the joyfulness you long to walk in each day. Rise up.

Prayer

Father,

Thank you for helping me walk a path of joy. Thank you for helping me be true to who I am. Amen.

Thank you for reading: Angel Guidance for Energy Healing. I hope you enjoyed the messages from the angels.

I want to give you a FREE gift before you go!

Please visit: http://eepurl.com/cV-Trf

For your free PDF copy of:

ANGEL GUIDANCE FOR WEALTH

By signing up, you'll receive a free book, angel messages, and new updates from Z.Z. Rae's works.

Author Bio

Z.Z. Rae is the author of 25 books and counting (fiction is under Natasha House.) Tagged in almost every unicorn post out there, Z.Z. loves the mystical, magical, and beautifully strange. As a child, she connected to God and relayed messages of love to people in her local community.

Now, as an adult Z.Z. channels God, angels, fairies, unicorns, and mermaids into her books. You can read direct messages from the angels in her Angel Guidance Series, and people have compared her energy to Doreen Virtue, "The Angel Lady."

An empath, oracle card reader, healer, speaker, and intuitive soul, Z.Z. helps people connect to their true, authentic self. Her FREE LIVE Facebook readings on Z.Z.'s Angel Card Corner get thousands of views.

If you'd like to find out more about Z.Z. Rae and her works come and stop by for a visit!

Facebook: Z.Z's Angel Card Corner

Blog: https://angelguidancetoday.wordpress.com/

Email: authorzzrae@gmail.com

If you've enjoyed this book, I would love for you to post a review. As an author, I am always learning and growing, and I'd love to hear back from you.

Made in the USA
Middletown, DE
21 December 2018